MENTAL HEALTH

for

GLOBAL MISSIONARIES

Patrick Sawyer
and
Cathy Napier

AUTHORS' NOTE:
80% of the proceeds from this book will be donated back to missions.

Table of Contents

CHAPTER ONE:
Mental Health
for Global Missionaries

Then He said to his disciples, "The harvest is plentiful, but the workers are few. Ask the Lord of the harvest, therefore, to send out workers into his harvest field."

(Matthew 9 vs. 37-38)

The calling came to both husband and wife simultaneously, as they prayed regarding their role in mission work, during a short-term mission to Nepal. Michael Seymour had been in the insurance business, and his wife Samantha Seymour had been a schoolteacher. Samantha prayed, "Lord, increase my sphere of influence for You." Michael prayed, "Lord, is this what You want me to do?"

They'd arrived in Nepal in July 2014. They were both excited and uncertain about quitting their jobs and heading to one of the most remote places in the world. It was a place noted for the beauty of Mount Everest, where men and women challenged themselves beyond the norm, climbing the world's highest peak of 29,000 feet to reach the summit. Everest stands in the Nepalese distance like a fine painting and was put there by none other than the most talented artist, our triune God, who can throw colors together like flowers of the field and have it work.

Michael and Samantha could identify with those who traveled to Nepal to climb the beautiful but dangerous Himalayas. They too had a challenge ahead of them—a calling to reach those who were deeply steeped in religions without the power of Jesus Christ. The Seymours had the desire to do this work, but also faced the mental dangers of depression, anxiety, trauma, and loneliness. These dangers can leave an imprint on a person's brain without their knowledge.

The trek to the Tengboche Monastery takes days. Michael described how the dirt road that is the only way to reach this destination is surrounded by dire poverty. One must hike through small villages inhabited by people having no access to clean water and food. This contrasts with the beauty of the area, with its panoramic view of the Himalayas.

While Michael and Samantha were in daily mission work for our Lord, they witnessed a world that was foreign to both of them. They experienced the earthquake that devastated parts of Nepal, witnessed poverty that was unlike any they had seen in the States, and worked in proximity to the huge Nepalese human-trafficking industry. With respect to the latter, Wikipedia states that the Nepal-India border is one of the busiest sites for human trafficking of girls from Nepal into India for forced prostitution. An estimated 5,000 to 10,000 Nepali women are trafficked to India each year.

Although such suffering is commonplace around the world now, for a missionary couple who has never been exposed to it, it is a lot to adjust to. Exposure to or knowledge of the current Sodom and Gomorrah world we live in can cause depression, anxiety, and burnout. Missionaries often experience a feeling of helplessness—especially, in the case of sex trafficking, when young women disappear with no explanation. Most new missionaries come from a long involvement with the church. They have been raised in a loving, caring Christian family with little to no problems. When the Lord calls them to the mission field, sometimes they are unprepared for what they experience.

Michael describes standing in what seemed like the middle of Nepal, with its beautiful backdrop and light surrounding him on every side. As he looked to the foothills of the surrounding mountains, he saw Hindu religious activity going on below—the burning of dead bodies, accompanied by a prayer to lead the dead into a cleansing ritual. The Hindu religion sees the body as made up of five elements—earth, water, fire, air, and space—and believes that it must be given back to those elements after death. Michael described the two-part terrain—the mountains and the ground below—as the spiritual divide between the backdrop of light behind him, as seen in the beauty and power of Everest, and the chasm below of dark, burned bodies, whose putrid odor entered his nostrils. This first snapshot of trauma had now been stamped in his brain permanently.

No one can prepare missionaries for what they may experience abroad, but the church can help with the aftermath, mentally and emotionally.

Begin to write down how you identify with Michael and Samantha. Use the journal page below to write your thoughts and feelings, using your own experience on the field. Identify a reaction to an experience that still bothers you. If you can identify the situations that continue leaving an imprint on your brain, then do so. Remember how Michael smelled the burning flesh of the burning bodies, and how he can still remember his mental aversion to that experience.

Journaling Pages

| 8 |

CHAPTER TWO:
What Does God Say About Missionary Service?

"Now there were in the church at Antioch prophets and teachers, Barnabas, Simeon who was called Niger, Lucius of Cyrene, Manaen a lifelong friend of Herod the tetrarch, and Saul. While they were worshiping the Lord and fasting, the Holy Spirit said, "Set apart for me Barnabas and Saul for the work to which I have called them." Then after fasting and praying they laid their hands on them and sent them off. (Acts 13:1-3)

In Acts 13, we see the church at Antioch fast, pray, lay hands on Paul and Barnabas, and send them to take the gospel of Jesus Christ to the nations. We believe the church at Antioch is a model for all churches to fulfill the Great Commission that Jesus gave us in Matthew 28, because in these verses we see the local church send its members to take the gospel to a world that desperately needs it.

Do not get us wrong, there are great parachurch organizations that God uses to send Christians all over the world for the sake of the gospel. But when it comes to fulfilling the Great Commission for that work, we believe this should ultimately be the responsibility of the local church. We also believe that as the local church sends its members into the mission field, it has a responsibility to care for them—before they go, while they are there, and even when they return.

David Wilson, in his book *Mind The Gaps,* states that the local church not only has a responsibility to *equip* its members to go into the field, but to *care* for them as well.[1] Why is this important? Ryan Martin, in his book *Holding The Rope*, states that "faithfulness to the task of the Great Commission is in direct correlation to our faithfulness to send and support well."[2] He goes on to say that "if churches begin caring for their missionaries long before they commission them, then they can better stabilize, support, and strengthen their sent ones' faithfulness to the task."[3]

In the article "Don't Just Be a Sending Church, Be a Staying Church," Aaron Menikoff states that it's not enough to be a sending church. A *staying* church doesn't let the rope fray, or the bond loosen. As inconvenient as the relationship may be, a staying church remains involved—by praying faithfully, communicating regularly, visiting occasionally, and always looking for new and creative ways to help. This is how we hold the rope, and we mustn't let go."[4] Churches that send and support well are more effective at helping to sustain their church members on the field, which leads to greater advancement of the gospel, which leads to more people hearing the gospel.[5]

---

1. David Wilson. *Mind The Gaps: Engaging the Church in Missionary Care* (Colorado Springs, CO: Believers, 2015).

2. Ryan Martin. *Holding The Rope: How the Local Church Can Care for its Sent Ones* (Knoxville, TN: Upstream, 2022), 17.

3. Ibid., 18.

4. Aaron Menikoff, "Don't Just Be Sending Church, Be a Staying Church", *Reaching and Teaching Blog,* 24 November 2020, http://rtim.org/dont-just-be-a-sending-church-be-a-staying-church/.

5. Ryan Martin. *Holding The Rope: How the Local Church Can Care for its Sent Ones*

One way that churches can care for their members who are on the mission field is by providing for their counseling needs. The truth is that missionaries on the field are going to face hard times. They are going to face suffering, persecution, loneliness, depression, failure, burnout, and trauma. We have spoken with many church planters and missionaries all over the world and hear over and over about these experiences.

Just within our local church, we have dealt with many of these issues from some of our partners on the field. We had one missionary couple who experienced threats and persecution. We had one missionary couple who experienced the death of a team member as well as civil unrest that forced them to quickly come out of the field. We had one church planter whose church leadership team tried to overthrow his leadership and remove him from the church.

Schaefer and Schaefer in 2012 revealed statistics gathered from fourteen West African countries where missionaries had suffered some type of trauma.[6] Of the male missionaries, 92% reported one or more severe traumas. Of the female missionaries, the figure was 85%. These can be further broken down into the following categories:

- 61% were due to serious illness
- 56% were due to car, train, or plane accidents
- 51% were due to the death of a family member or close friend
- 48% were due to fighting, civil unrest, or war
- 41% were due to burglary
- 38% were due to a serious threat or harm to a family member or close friend

---

(Knoxville, TN: Upstream, 2022), 19.

6. Faruke C. Schaefer and Charles A. Schaefer. *Trauma and Resilience: Effectively Supporting those who Serve God*-A Handbook. Condeo Press, 2012

- 34% were due to seeing another person seriously injured or killed
- 31% were due to evacuation

An example of a specific mission that resulted in depression, anxiety, and trauma was the mission of a war hero we will call Brad. I compare the war hero with that of a missionary because both serve God, country, and protect a people. Both can suffer from depression, anxiety, and depression. Brad was taken by ambulance to a Dallas hospital after attending a ballgame in the old Texas Rangers Stadium in Arlington, Texas (before the modern stadium that was the brainchild of President George W. Bush when he was governor). Brad was out on a hot Texas afternoon with some of his buddies, enjoying the game and having a few beers. He went to the bathroom, and the next thing he knew, he was being taken to a local emergency room, where it was determined he needed intensive inpatient care. So, an ambulance took him to a Dallas hospital's psychiatric ward.

One of the authors of this workbook, Cathy Napier, was assigned the patient. In a case as severe as Brad's, one must go on a fact-finding mission. How does a successful businessman, husband, and father of three experience a complete breakdown? The treatment team works from a biopsychosocial assessment. Now, you may ask why this context is important. But if a loved one is dealing with depression and anxiety, this knowledge is helpful. Brad had been in Vietnam, and his job was to fly out in a helicopter to recover the dead bodies of our soldiers who lost their lives in battle.

In therapy sessions, Cathy helped Brad connect the dots. Brad had repressed the memory of picking up dead bodies, but his brain remembered the smell of his traumatic work. When trauma leaves an imprint on our psyche, we can often push it down, but the brain continues to remember. When Brad entered the ballpark bathroom on that hot summer day, it became a perfect mental storm. His brain connected the smell of the bathroom—especially feces and urine—with the trauma he experienced during his Vietnam missions, which were marked by the same stench. Thus, the bathroom triggered a trauma response.

When Brad had returned from Vietnam, he went straight to work supporting his wife and expecting a child. He didn't receive counseling after Vietnam; nor did he feel that he needed it. Given all the years that had elapsed since he'd been in Vietnam, why was the experience of war starting to cause Brad problems now? He was having marital problems, difficulty with a teenage son, and business problems due to a downturn in the economy. His coping skills had begun to crack, intensifying his stress. These factors are a perfect storm for surfacing repressed trauma.

Cathy was ultimately able to help him connect the dots. Knowledge is power.

Does everyone who has trauma experience the same thing Brad did? Not necessarily, but past trauma can cause an anxious feeling. If your anxiety and fear are elevated, please see a Christian counselor for help to work through what's causing that. God is not the author of fear. God has given us a sound mind. Not everyone has the same intense trauma that Brad experienced, but everyone has *some* type of trauma in their lifetime. A given trauma can't inherently be characterized as mild, moderate, or severe—each person's trauma affects them differently. As Christians, we are to bear one another's burdens, so having Christian fellowship where we can share and ask for prayer is extremely important for our mental health. Brad had little, if any, counseling to deal with the trauma of Vietnam. This is the case for many coming home from war. A lack of counseling can be the case for missionaries coming off the mission field with a lack of resources to help them deal with what they have experienced negatively.

Brad left the service, got married, had children, and started a business. He felt there was no time to look back at his experiences in

Vietnam. Not everyone who puts off dealing with trauma like this will experience the kind of resurgence that Brad did. But it is never good to bury trauma, anger, or depression. One should deal with it—otherwise, it will come out in various ways.

Brad's mission as a soldier was similar to the work of church missionaries. He defended our country and protected the rights of the vulnerable, including people who have no belief system but view America as a land that states, "In God we Trust." Missionaries serve our God to help those who are vulnerable due to poverty, political unrest, or lack of exposure to the gospel.

Use the lines below to list or journal about the similarities you may have with Brad after re-entry into your homeland. Pay special attention to incidents that may have left an indelible imprint on your brain.

____

____

____

____

____

____

CHAPTER THREE:
Missionary Re-entry

In our journey toward wellness, we will regularly refer to the two case studies we've just introduced: Michael and Samantha Seymour, and Brad. We'll compare their missionary journeys to that of the Apostle Paul. We will use the word of God along with best practice therapies to provide a protocol for healing on missionary "re-entry," or return to the home society.

In Acts 13, we see the church at Antioch send out Paul and Barnabas to take the gospel of Jesus Christ to the Gentile nations. Paul and Barnabas would then take the gospel to Cyprus, Pisidia, Iconium, Lystra, Pamphylia, Perga, and Attalia. In Acts 14, we see that after they passed through Attalia, they sailed back to Antioch. Verses 26–28 states that "from there they sailed to Antioch, where they had been commended to the grace of God for the work that they had fulfilled. And when they arrived and gathered the church together, they declared all that God had done with them, and how he had opened a door of faith to the Gentiles. And they remained no little time with the discipled."

We do not know exactly how long Paul and Barnabas were in Antioch, but according to Scripture, after being on the field, they returned home for a period. You will see going forward how the Apostle Paul had difficulty each time he was out and on his journey. You will read more about the two missions introduced above—the Seymours, serving in Nepal, and Brad, serving his country in Vietnam. You will see the comparison between these missions and the missionary journey of Paul. You will develop psychological tools to use with the scriptures to overcome anxiety, stress, depression, loneliness, and trauma. Churches that send those who are called out to the field should consider using a plan for mental healthcare in global missions, so these laborers in the field can be prepared.

Churches would also be wise to use this workbook as a missionary re-entry plan. Most missionaries will eventually come off the field. Sometimes it's temporary, as with a furlough; sometimes it's permanent, because of retirement, failure, burnout, or some other reason. Neal Pirolo, in his book *The Reentry Team*, states that "there are various reasons for missionaries to come home from their fields of service before the end of their term of commitment. The tragedy of human experience brings some home. Others return for reasons of discontent on the field. Still others discover that they should never have gone to the field in the first place!"[7] The point is that missionaries will more than likely come off the field at some point and local churches should be ready and equipped to care for them and help them with re-entry. Yet, as Pirolo states, "the churches have a lack of knowledge of the issues missionaries face on reentry."[8]

One tool of our spiritual enemy is depression. Depression paralyzes. If we're paralyzed, we can't be effective. Paul describes many feelings on his historic missionary journey that lead us to believe he became extremely depressed. "For we do not want you to be unaware, brothers, of the affliction we experienced in Asia," he notes in 2 Corinthians 1:8. "For we were so utterly burdened beyond

---

7. Neal Pirolo, *The Reentry Team: Caring For Your Returning Missionaries* (San Diego, CA: Emmaus Road International, 2000), 242.

8. Neal Pirolo, *The Reentry Team: Caring For Your Returning Missionaries* (San Diego, CA: Emmaus Road International, 2000), 19.

our strength that we despaired of life itself." As Paul was reflecting on his life and ministry and all the hardships he had experienced, he became overwhelmed with emotion. He reveals that he even thought about wanting to die. The word "despair" means the complete absence of hope. Scripture does not reveal what happened during Paul's journey to Asia, but Paul felt an utter loss; he was crushed so badly that he could not get up.

Kent Hughes says, "Paul sensed that despite all his remarkable earlier deliverances, his time had come. Think of it! Paul had had multiple life-threatening experiences—the stoning, five beatings that each took him to within an inch of his life, multiple dangers, and shipwrecks. But this affliction in Asia was the most damaging and also debilitating. An inexorable, paralyzing weight had fallen on him in Asia, and there was no exit."

One of the greatest Baptist preachers, Charles Spurgeon, suffered greatly from depression, too. Spurgeon stated, "I have suffered many times from severe sickness and frightful mental depression seeking almost despair. Almost every year I've been laid aside for a season, for flesh and blood cannot bear the strain, at least such flesh and blood as mine. I believe, however, the affliction was necessary to me and has answered salutary ends."[9]

During Spurgeon's ministry, he dealt with many issues that led to his depression. First, when he was twenty-two years old, he was preaching for the first time in the Music Hall of the Royal Surrey Gardens, and during his sermon someone from the crowd yelled "fire," causing a stampede, which led to the death of seven people. Spurgeon almost quit the ministry over this tragedy, and the incident would continue to haunt him with post-traumatic stress, and feelings

---

9. Excepted from Randy Alcorn's foreword to Charles Spurgeon, *Encouragement for the Depression.*

of guilt and responsibility.[10] Over the course of his ministry, Spurgeon personally dealt with smallpox, gout, rheumatism, and Bright's disease (inflammation of the kidneys). Because of these health issues, he was out of the pulpit nearly a third of his last twenty-two years.[11]

Spurgeon knew the truth that in pastoral ministry, we will have hard times. We will suffer. He stated that "our work, when earnestly undertaken, lays us open to attacks in the direction of depression. Who can bear the weight of souls without sometimes sinking to the dust? Passionate longings after men's conversion, if not fully satisfied, consume the soul with anxiety and disappointment. To see the hopeful turn aside, the godly grow cold, professors abusing their privileges, and sinners waxing more bold sin—are not these sights enough to crush us to the earth? How often, on Lord's day evenings, do we feel as if life were completely washed out of us! After pouring out our souls over our congregations, we feel like the empty earthen pitchers which a child might break".[12]

How did Spurgeon endure suffering and depression? In his book *Lectures to My Students*, Spurgeon says, "I daresay the greatest earthly blessing that God can give to any of us is health, with the exception of sickness. If some men whom I know could only be favored with a month of rheumatism, it would, by God's grace, mellow them marvelously."[13] The reason Spurgeon was able to endure through suffering and depression was because it drew him closer to God. Spurgeon believed

----

10. Zach Erswine, "Charles Spurgeon (1834-92): Faithful in Sorrow," in *12 Faithful Men*, edited by Colin Hansen and Jeff Robinson (Grand Rapids: Baker, 2018), 131.

11. Justin Taylor, "Charles Spurgeon Battle with Depression" in *The Gospel Coalition*, May 19, 2022.

12. Justin Taylor, "Charles Spurgeon Battle with Depression" in *The Gospel Coalition*, May 19, 2022.

13. Charles Spurgeon, *An All Around Ministry* (Independently Published, 2017), 384.

the Lord allows us to endure suffering to draw us closer to Him so we will not only understand our frailty, but also our constant need and dependence on Him. Spurgeon stated, "I am afraid that all the grace I have got of my comfortable and easy times and happy hours might almost lie on a penny. But the good I have received from my sorrows and pains and griefs is altogether incalculable. Affliction is the best book in a minister's library."[14]

Spurgeon also found comfort in God's Word—for instance, in verses such as Matthew 5:11 ("Blessed are you, when others revile you and persecute you and utter all kinds of evil against you falsely on my account") and Isaiah 48:10 ("Behold, I have refined you, but not as silver; I have tried you in the furnace of affliction"). The word of Scripture and the stories of people in the Bible kept him encouraged. In his book the *Chequebook of the Bank of Faith*, he stated, "I believe all the promises of God, but many of them I have personally tried and proved. I would say to fellow Christians in their trials; My brethren, God is good. He will not forsake you: He will bear you through. Everything else will fail, but His Word never will."[15]

Spurgeon and Depression Continued

In the book *Spurgeon's Sorrow*, Zack Eswine reveals five truths about depression according to Spurgeon.[16]

- Man is made up of both body and soul and both can be hurt.

---

14. Justin Taylor, "Charles Spurgeon Battle with Depression" in *The Gospel Coalition*, May 19, 2022.

15. Diana Gruver, "Charles Spurgeon Knew It Was Possible to be Faithful and Depressed" in *Christianity Today,* February 26, 2012.

16. Zack Eswine, *Spurgeon's Sorrows: Realistic Hope for those who Suffer from Depression* (Scotland: UK, Christian Focus, 2007), 37-40.

• Depression is not a sin. Spurgeon states, "We may get depressed in spirit; we may be nervous, fearful, timid; we may almost come to the borders of despair and this apart from sin."[17]

• We are not alone in depression. There are numerous examples in Scripture and church history of other Christians struggling with depression. Martin Luther, Isaac Newton, William Cowper, Job, King David, Elijah, and Jesus. Spurgeon states, "You are not the first child of God who has been depressed or troubled. Even among the noblest of men and women who ever lived, there has been much of this kind of thing. Do not, therefore, think that you are quite alone in your sorrow."[18]

• We may not be fully cured from depression on this side of heaven. According to Spurgeon, "we do not profess that the religion of Christ will so thoroughly change a man as to take away from him all his natural tendencies; it will give the despairing something that will alleviate that despondency, but as long as that is caused by a low state of body, or a diseased mind, we do not profess that the religion of Christ will totally remove it. No, rather, we do see every day that amongst the best of God's servants, there are those who are always doubting, always looking to the dark side of every providence, who look at the threatening more than at the promise, who are easy to write bitter things against themselves."[19]

---

17. Charles Spurgeon, "Our Youth Renewed," *MTP*, Vol. 60 (Ages Digital Library, 1998), 462.

18. Charles Spurgeon, "The Cause and Cure of a Wounded Spirit", *MTP,* Vol. 42 (Ages Digital Library, 1998), 791-792.

19. Charles Spurgeon, "Weak Hands and Feeble Knees," *NPSP* Sermon 243 in the Spurgeon

- God comforts us through depression. In Spurgeon's view, "some of you may be in great distress of mind, a distress out of which no fellow creature can deliver you. You are a poor nervous person at whom others often laugh. I can assure you that God will not laugh at you; he knows all about sad complaints of yours, so I urge you to go to him, for the experience of many of us has taught us the Lord is gracious and full of compassion."[20]

How did Spurgeon recommend dealing with depression? He proposed two types of help: *spiritual* and *natural*.

Spiritual help involves the following:

- Finding comfort in Jesus. Hebrews 4:15 states, "For we do not have a high priest who is unable to sympathize with our weaknesses, but one who in every respect has been tempted as we are, yet without sin." Spurgeon indicates that in the Garden of Gethsemane Jesus experienced depression as he sweated blood and prayed to the Father to remove the cup of God's wrath from him. Christians suffering from depression can find comfort in Jesus because He knows what they are going through—He experienced it.

- Find comfort in the promises of God's Word, such as Psalm 91:4 ("He will cover you with his feathers, and under his wings you will find refuge"). Spurgeon posted Scripture throughout his home as a reminder of God's

---

Archive (http://www.spurgeon.org/sermons/0243.htm), accessed 12/13/13.

20. Charles Spurgeon, "Remembering God's Works", *MTP*, Vol. 49 (Ages Digital Library, 1998), 591.

promises. Eswine notes that "in Spurgeon's bedroom they had framed Matthew 5:11-12, "blessed are you, when others revile you, and persecute you, and utter all kinds of evil against you falsely on my account. Rejoice and be glad, for your reward is great in heaven, for so they persecuted the prophets who were before you".[21] One promise that Spurgeon continuously referred to in prayer was Psalm 103:13: "As a father shows compassion to his children, so the Lord shows compassion to those who fear him."

Natural help was another method Spurgeon used for dealing with depression. In his view, it had the following components:

Laughter

Consider Proverbs 17:22: "a joyful heart is good medicine." Spurgeon believed in the power of laughter when suffering depression. He stated, "cheerfulness readily carries burdens."[22]

Rest and Retreats

Spurgeon points out that "beyond all medicine, stimulant, cordial, or lecturing . . . I commend quiet hours in calm retreats."[23] Spurgeon spent time in Mentone, France for rest

---

21. Zack Eswine, *Spurgeon's Sorrows: Realistic Hope for those who Suffer from Depression* (Scotland: UK, Christian Focus, 2007), 95.

22. Charles Spurgeon, "Bells for the Horses," *MTP* (http://www.spurgeon.org/s_and _t/ bells.htm), accessed 3/19/14.

23. Ibid.

and recovery when he experienced deep depression.[24] Each year he also got away from the winter into the sunshine. Psychologist believe the removal of a patient from their everyday cares and stresses can have positive effects against depression.[25]

Medicine

Spurgeon also believed in the power and importance of medicine. He stated, "it would not be wise to live by a supposed faith, and cast off the physician and his medicine, any more than to discharge the butcher, and the tailor, and expect to be fed and clothed by faith."[26] In addition to God's Word, prayer, and rest, Spurgeon also believed in the power of medicine.

24. Zack Eswine, *Spurgeon's Sorrows: Realistic Hope for those who Suffer from Depression* (Scotland: UK, Christian Focus, 2007), 108.

25. Bucknill, *A Manuel of Psychological Medicine*, 500.

26. Charles, Spurgeon, "Beloved and Yet Afflicted," Sermon 1518 ((http://www.spurgeon. org/sermons/1518.htm), accessed 3/14/14.

Journaling Pages

1. Describe and journal those things that you feel could be a factor in your depression.

2. Make a list of those things you can do to help with your depression.

CHAPTER FOUR:
God-Given Brain

In doing this series on depression, anxiety, and trauma, we would like to focus on how the brain works. The brain is an organ that must be exercised. We must continue using it—or, like anything else that's not used, it will atrophy. Thankfully, God's word has something to say about the human mind. As Christians, we have access to the mind of Jesus Christ, which has a spiritual and a practical aspect.

The Greek term for mind is *nous*. It refers to the human mind, mental activity, the total inner or moral attitude, and understanding or thinking ability.[27] We see this term used in Romans 12:2a: "Do not be conformed to this world but be transformed by the renewal of your mind." Our lives are impacted by the way we think. In one sense, the term *nous* represents our inner moral consciousness, which directs the decisions we make.[28] Thus, if we want to make decisions that honor God, we must spend time in His word, recalibrating our inner moral consciousness.

Reading God's word renews our minds and realigns our will with God's. Interestingly, the apostle Paul wrote to the church at Corinth,

---

27. Gerhard Kittel, ed., *Theological Dictionary of the New Testament IV* (Grand Rapids: Eerdmans, 2006), 952-53.

28. Ibid., 958.

"But we have the mind of Christ."[29] What did Paul mean by this? When we become Christians, is there a surgical process that gives us a divine mind? No, that is *not* what Paul meant.

Rather, in the context of 1 Corinthians, Paul distinguished between the *natural man* and the *spiritual man*. The natural man is a person who has not trusted in Jesus Christ for salvation. This person does not accept spiritual truth because it does not make sense. Concepts like sin, a Trinitarian God, heaven, hell, etc., seem like fantasy and are not understood. Paul wrote that spiritual truths are spiritually discerned and can only be grasped by someone with the Holy Spirit. We receive the Holy Spirit when we place our faith in Jesus Christ alone for salvation. Without the Holy Spirit, we do not have the mind of Jesus.[30] So the scriptures are correct—we can use our God-given mind to help us learn to deal with the depression, anxiety, and trauma we're exposed to on the mission field.

There is also a practical component to having the mind of Jesus Christ. In Philippians 2, Paul instructed the church at Philippi in humility to count others as more important than themselves (verse 3). Then, in verse 5, he wrote, "Have this mind among yourselves, which is yours in Christ Jesus." Christians should deny themselves and consider others as more important—just like Jesus did when He laid down His life to pay for the world's sins.

The missionary's total surrender to Christ enables them to put others' needs first, and there's a consequence to doing that. Our human nature is to put ourselves first. The missionary is going to feel lonely, depressed, and drained by putting their needs last. That's exactly what the missionary signs up for—just like Brad, who had to put the protection of the South Vietnamese people first instead of his own. So, whatever anxiety, trauma, or depression he experienced at the time had

---

29. 1 Corinthians 2:16.

30. *TDNT IV*, 959.

to be put on hold. Re-entry for Brad could have been different if he'd had several weeks of re-entry counseling. Similarly, missionaries forced to resign from service might have had a better re-entry if they'd been given several weeks of sound spiritual counseling by their churches.

Next, we'll look at the brain to explain why Michael, Samantha, and Brad had some residual trauma from their service.

How the Brain Works

The brain is one big computer bank that records and stores many of our experiences and events. When a newborn comes into the world they cannot see for some time. The newborn learns to navigate the world through their senses. Jordan Rosenfeld states that a four-week-old fetus forms new neurons at a rate of 250,000 every minute, and trillions of connections will be built with each experience. Some we remember, and some are computed by our brain and filed away. We may not remember, but our senses correlate what we see, smell, and hear, and they mark the experience, either good or bad. That's why sometimes you smell a pleasant smell and have a warm fuzzy feeling but don't remember why. The same is true when you have a bad reaction to a smell or sight—even if, again, you can't remember *why*.

The Phoenix Society for Burn Survivors has explained the way our brain works when traumatized. When a person experiences something traumatic, adrenalin and other neurochemicals rush to the brain and print a picture there. The traumatic memory loops in the emotional side of the brain, disconnecting from the part of the brain that conducts reasoning and cognitive processing. The rational part of the brain is unable to help the emotionally loaded part of the brain create distance from the trauma. The chemicals released target and intensify our emotions: depression, anxiety, fear, loneliness, etc. All these emotions result from the trauma we're experiencing. Once the trauma is dealt with, then perhaps the depression, anxiety, fear, and loneliness will also disappear.

The Phoenix Society explains, in a way a layman can understand, why a person sometimes reacts to outside stimuli without being able to connect the dots with the trauma they're experiencing. In understanding how the brain and body function during trauma, we look at the parts of the brain such as the prefrontal cortex, the limbic system (which is located in the center of the brain), and the brain stem. When a person experiences trauma, adrenaline rushes through the body and the memory is imprinted into the amygdala, which is part of the limbic system. The amygdala holds the emotional significance of the event—including the intensity and impulse of emotion that directs a person to fight or flight.

Therefore, the visual images of trauma are not stored like a story, but rather as sensory fragments—i.e., how our five senses experienced the trauma at the time it occurred. These memories can be stored through fragments of sights, smells, sounds, tastes, or touch.

If your trauma is a conscious memory, can you journal it as you may have experienced while on the mission field? Use the space below to write down images that cause anxiety or that you feel may be a part of your trauma.

Consider the stress and anxiety a missionary feels as they return to their pre-field home, exacerbated by the weight of depression and unknown trauma. They can feel stress and anxiety from leaving the field. They may have stress and anxiety from leaving friends made on the field—maybe neighbors, or those they have been ministering to. One missionary couple we spoke with *had* to come off the field because they were exposed by the government. Being forced to leave made them very sad. They had to leave long-time friendships they had developed over the years.

A protocol for stress and anxiety is meditating on scripture. Memorize these scriptures so you can have them with you always. Use scripture I Peter 5 vs. 6 -7: "Humble yourselves, therefore, under God's mighty hand, that he may lift you up in due time. Cast all your anxiety on him because he cares for you. Imagine yourself with God's hand over you and releasing your anxiety to him. In Matthew chapter II, vs. 30, Jesus says, "my yolk is easy and my burden is light." This is where you can get off to yourself, do some deep diaphragm breathing, and release your anxiety to our Lord and savior.

Another cause of stress and anxiety for missionaries coming off the field is when they must leave a ministry they have invested a good deal of time in. The couple who had to leave their current country were sad because they had to leave a ministry they had sacrificed for and worked hard to develop over many years. Think about a missionary couple who is retiring. You can imagine the stress and anxiety they might experience coming to terms with the fact that their ministry is over. It's the same with any career. When people retire after working many years, they can develop stress and anxiety because they don't know what life will look like tomorrow. Missionaries who are done with ministry forever can develop stress not knowing what their life will look like tomorrow as well.

Yet another cause of stress and anxiety for missionaries coming off the field is trauma from persecution or governmental unrest. We knew one missionary couple from the Middle East who experienced persecution, so they had to come off the field for a period to let things settle down. Another missionary couple experienced governmental unrest, and their ministry decided to shut down their ministry, which had been active for a century. This family had to leave friends and a ministry they had poured themselves into for many years.

Then there is the unbelievable stress caused when missionaries come off the field because they are unable to continue or are burned out. This stress is due to believing they have failed God, family, friends, their church, other churches, or people who have supported them. This can carry an enormous amount of weight.

It is not only leaving the field that causes stress and anxiety—stress and anxiety is also caused when a missionary moves back to their original culture. First, there is the *physical* stress—traveling long distances with family or alone is an exhausting process that can involve everything from jet lag to lost baggage to layovers to delays to uncomfortable plane rides.

There is also professional stress. When a missionary comes off the field permanently, they more than likely will need to find some other career to engage in. They can develop stress and anxiety from having to find a job and scrambling to provide for their family. Some missionaries who come off the field feel their ministry is not over, so they develop anxiety waiting on what their next assignment may be from the Lord. One missionary couple who was forced to come off the field felt their ministry was not done—they had to come off the field and wait until the Lord gave them their next assignment. They trusted God, but they had no idea how long they'd have to wait and where God might lead them next.

Missionaries coming off the field must move back into a new culture. Think about the stress and anxiety that comes from moving from a slower, relational culture (familiar culture) to a more fast-paced and time-oriented culture, or vice versa. This can take the form of national, political, or legal challenges. Imagine moving to a new world with unfamiliar laws that you must adapt to. When Patrick, one of the authors of this book, went to Nepal on a short-term trip, he felt stressed and overwhelmed just dealing with the country's driving laws. He'd come from a country where there were streetlights and stop signs and traveled to a country where there were none.

There might be educational stress, too. Lots of missionaries homeschool their children while on the field. What if, when they come off the field, they decide to put their children into the public school system? Imagine how stressful this can be for parents. It's stressful enough for most parents when their children start a new year within the same school. Just imagine starting at a new school in a new country.

We mustn't forget that there is also spiritual stress. A missionary on the field pours their entire lives into engaging a new culture with the gospel of Jesus Christ. Moving back to their home culture, they might feel lost, spiritually. They might even struggle with what God wants them to do now that they are no longer on the field. This can be very intense and demanding. They can wander around feeling disconnected from their local church, or even lost to ministry.

As missionaries re-enter their original culture and face these overwhelming causes of stress, you can imagine how they react. Some may experience denial. Some may believe they are immune. Some may say, "It will never happen to me." Some may experience alienation and isolation.

Pirolo describes a typical experience of these returning missionaries: "He may feel there is no one to talk to, no one who could possibly understand, no one to help him process his thoughts."[31] Some may experience anger and resentment. Some can become angry at their home culture. Consider the ramifications. A missionary returning from

31. Neal Pirolo, *The Reentry Team: Caring For Your Returning Missionaries* (San Diego, CA: Emmaus Road International, 2000), 43.

a relational (familiar) and hospitable culture may become frustrated and angry at their home culture, which might be more time and task oriented.

One of the authors of this study knew a missionary whose family had been on the mission field for many years, and when they returned to America, they did not like the lifestyle that America had come to favor. They easily became frustrated and angry. This is a form of cultural stress. There's a period of overstimulation for those returning from a country where they've witnessed dire poverty or desperate immigrants escaping a war-torn country (for instance, missionaries in Moldova, who have witnessed those leaving Ukraine for the trek to Moldova). Returning to the US, where they have lived a life of plenty, can challenge their values. They might have questions, like "Where do I belong?" Or, "How can I become comfortable again after what I have witnessed?" These thoughts are normal, but intrusive. They can be accompanied by hidden trauma responses that only the brain remembers.

Some missionaries become depressed and even suicidal. Given all the differences in their new culture, they may eventually become so broken that they believe the only way out is suicide. In the movie *Shawshank Redemption*, there was a prisoner named Brooks, who was released from prison after many years, moved into a small apartment, and started working at a local grocery store. But Brooks became lost in a world that had changed so much that he thought his only option was to commit suicide. Missionaries who come off the field can become lost, too—they are often rejoining a world that has changed so much that they believe the only way out is suicide. Pirolo states that "the whirlwind of emotions leaves him broken. He backs out of life spiritually, mentally, emotionally, or he finds the ultimate escape of physical suicide his only alternative."[32]

---

32. Neal Pirolo, *The Reentry Team: Caring For Your Returning Missionaries* (San Diego, CA: Emmaus Road International, 2000), 45.

Write a description of your depression, and a timeline that includes when it started. If you can relate it to an incident you experienced while on the mission field, then do so.

Up to half of first-time missionaries return home early, and many don't return at all to the field.[33] Pirolo indicates that "these wounded people need to identify and process the hurt and anger of failure—to begin to build up their lives again, growing toward mental, emotional, and spiritual wholeness."[34] The truth is as churches develop a care plan for their missionaries as they leave and while they are on the field, it is just as important to have a plan for reentry. Pirolo states that "if a church has buy-in with sending a missionary to the field and supporting them on the field, then they should also receive that missionary home from the field in a hospitable way".[35]

Protocol for training missionaries for reentry after time on the mission field can include cognitive behavioral therapy (CBT). CBT is a psycho-social intervention that focuses on changing thoughts, beliefs, attitudes, and behaviors, from unhelpful to helpful. It also includes emotional regulation and coping strategies to solve problematic issues. Aaron Beck, a psychiatrist, developed this exercise. We use it in a way that is aligned with the word of God and can provide relief from depression, anxiety, and the effects of trauma. Depression, anxiety, and trauma are like physical diseases that if left untreated can get worse. CBT has been proven to be effective in treating mild to moderate levels of depression.

CBT is a type of psychotherapy that modifies thought patterns to help change moods and behaviors. It is a blend of cognitive and behavioral therapy. Cognitive therapy focuses on your moods and thoughts. Behavioral therapy specifically targets actions and behaviors. In your journal, you will break down reactions and thought patterns

---

33. Neal Pirolo, *Serving as Senders Today: How to Care for your Missionaries as they Prepare to Go, are on the Field and Return Home* (San Diego, CA: Emmaus Road International, 2012), 136.

34. Ibid.

35. Neal Pirolo, *The Reentry Team: Caring For Your Returning Missionaries* (San Diego, CA: Emmaus Road International, 2000), 26.

into several categories of self-defeating thought (also known as cognitive distortions).

These may include:

- All-or-nothing thinking: viewing the world in absolute, black-and-white terms. This is why you must practice question #2

- Disqualifying the positive: rejecting positive experiences. This is why you must become familiar with questions # 1, 3, and 4

- Automatic negative reactions: having habitual, scolding thoughts about yourself. This is why you must work through question #1

- Magnifying or minimizing the importance of an event: making a bigger or smaller deal about an event or moment than is necessary.

- Overgeneralization: drawing overly broad conclusions from a single event.

- Personalization: taking things too personally or feeling actions are specifically directed at you.

- Mental filter: picking out a single negative detail and dwelling on it so that your vision of reality becomes darkened. This is why you must again practice question #2.

In using your workbook you will be able to write down negative thought patterns or perceptions as well as constructive ones. This can be done through a series of well-practiced techniques, such as:

- Learning to manage and modify distorted thoughts and reactions.

- Learning to accurately and comprehensively assess external situations and your own reactions and emotional behavior.

- Practicing self-talk that is accurate and balanced.

- Using self-evaluation to reflect and respond appropriately.

You can practice these coping methods on your own or with a therapist.

How can CBT help with depression? It can't if you have a chemical imbalance, but if your depression is due to circumstances you've experienced on the mission field, then CBT can help you reframe your thoughts more constructively. It can help you uncover unhealthy patterns of thought and identify how they may be affecting your mood, your beliefs about yourself, and your outlook on life.

Journaling Pages

| 43 |

1. Write down a recurring negative thought or example of faulty thinking, especially as it pertains to your experience of reentry. For example, if your missionary work was in an area where you were surrounded by poverty, reentry into the opulence of America might have been difficult, making you feel guilty that you can live freely and enjoy a lifestyle that the people you served can only dream about.

____

____

____

____

____

____

____

____

____

2. Write down various ways you can reframe faulty thinking that can cause depression, anxiety, and trauma. For example, stay in the reality of each situation, acknowledging your senses by noting what you see, hear, taste, smell, and touch. When on the mission field, acknowledge these senses, and do the same when you return to your homeland. This will help you categorize each place and learn to live there in harmony. Do this exercise immediately upon reentry from the mission field and again when returning to the mission field. Be specific when writing these details down. For example, if you smelled something similar to what Michael smelled (the burning flesh described in an earlier chapter), and know it will stay with you, write it down so you can distinguish between what was in the mission field and what is back in your homeland.

3. How has a negative thought (or sequence of them) dictated your behavior since returning from the mission field?

4. How can reframing your negative thoughts into something more positive help you become more adjusted in returning to your homeland?

CHAPTER FIVE:
Anxiety Treatment for Missionaries and the People They Serve

We are addressing re-entry for those who have been embattled from their work on the mission field. Also we are addressing anxiety experienced by those with whom our missionaries serve. Anxiety can increase or simply appear without warning due to some type of trauma experienced while spending several months or years in a remote place where political unrest is witnessed, disease, and poverty like never witnessed before. Below we hope this will give some understanding of the disease of anxiety and how it can be overcome.

Anxiety is a feeling of worry, nervousness, or unease, typically about an imminent event or something with an uncertain outcome. If we are honest, all of us have experienced anxiety at some point in life.

The anxious life is the heavy life; it is a life weighed down with burdens. Proverbs 12:25 says, "Anxiety in a man's heart weighs him down, but a good word makes him glad." Interestingly, the term used in Proverbs 12:25 for anxiety, *de'agah*, includes the presence of fear, and means *anxious fear*.[36]

Yet, according to God's word, Christians are commanded, "Do not

---

36. NET Bible note no.78.

be anxious about anything."[37] The term Paul used for anxiety in its most basic sense means to care for someone or something, to have a careful or anxious concern for someone or something.[38] That definition seems harmless enough. So, why would Paul command Christians not to care about something or someone? In Luke 10, a lawyer asked Jesus what he could do to inherit eternal life. Jesus responded with what has become known as the parable of the Good Samaritan.

Jesus asked the man what was written in the Law and how he read it. The man responded, "You shall love the Lord your God with all your heart and with all your soul and with all your strength and with all your mind, and your neighbor as yourself."[39] In other words, as God's people we should love ourselves. Part of loving and caring for ourselves means meeting our daily physical needs, such as food, shelter, and clothing. But we also have spiritual and emotional needs that need addressing through time with God—in reading and prayer and relationships with others.

How are we supposed to love and care for ourselves without also living with anxiety? The key is to remember that, for Christians, life is not all about the here and now. We must remember the words of Jesus to Pilate; "My kingdom is not of this world."[40] Our life on earth is real, but so is heaven. Jesus ascended into heaven, as related in Acts 1:9, and has gone to prepare a place for His followers. One day he will return in the same way He went up to heaven.[41] When Jesus returns, He will take His people to be with Him and so we will always be with the Lord.[42] At that point, we will spend the rest of eternity in the presence of Jesus. But in the meantime, we live on this earth and face the cares of a world

---

37. Philippians 4:6.

38. Bultmann, *Theological Dictionary of the New Testament IV*, ed. Gerhard Kittel (Grand Rapids, Eerdmans, 2006), 589.

39. Luke 10:27.

40. John 18:36

41. John 14:3, Acts 1:11.

42. 1 Thessalonians 4:17.

impacted by sin. This is why Paul reminded the believers at Philippi that our citizenship is in heaven, and we await a Savior, the Lord Jesus Christ.[43] Christians have dual citizenship; we live as citizens of a particular country and as citizens of heaven.

This is in direct opposition to unbelievers in Jesus, whom Paul referred to as "enemies of the cross of Christ."[44] Unbelievers are characterized by minds fixed only on this world, because that is all they know. Christians must not live this way, and that is why Paul commanded Christians not to be anxious about anything. Christians must live considering their dual citizenship. When Christians are tempted to care too much about the things of the world, becoming anxious, Paul said they should pray "in everything by prayer and supplication with thanksgiving," letting their "requests be made known to God."[45]

The answer to anxiety is prayer because prayer transfers our anxiety to God. We transfer our anxious care to our heavenly Father who loves us. Without transferring our anxiety to God we will become consumed with it, our actions revealing we are living for this world rather than for heaven.[46] Living for God and for heaven means "casting all your anxieties on Him because he cares for you."[47] Casting our anxieties upon God is an act of trust because we are acting in obedience to His word and trusting that He will answer our requests according to His perfect will.

Finally, it is important to recognize that depression/anxiety/trauma interact with one another, often at the same time.

---

43. Philippians 3:20.

44. Philippians 3:18.

45. Philippians 4:6.

46. *TDNT IV*, 592.

47. 1 Peter 5:7.

CHAPTER SIX:
Removing Anxiety with Rational Emotive Therapy (RET)

We know that anxiety causes stress, and stress causes anxiety.

But as is noted in Philippians 4:6, "Do not be anxious about anything, but present your requests to God in everything. And the peace of God."

QUESTIONS

List those things that are causing you to stress since returning from the mission field.

____

____

____

____

____

List the stressful situations that you have no control over.

____

____

____

____

____

____

____

____

____

____

____

____

____

After listing the things that are stressful that you have no control over, practice the serenity prayer by Reinhold Niebuhr, as a mantra: "God, help me to accept the things I can not change, the courage to change the things I can, and the wisdom to know the difference."

List the stressful situations that you can control.

How have your anxiety-producing stressors affected you physically? Please explain.

Have your stressors caused your depression?

Has your anxiety caused you to have a panic attack (either once or repeatedly)? If you can, try and remember these events in detail, then write them out below.

CHAPTER SEVEN:
RET for Stress
and/or Phobias
That Can Cause Anxiety
and Panic Attacks

Refer to Albert Ellis's Rational Emotive Therapy (RET). Then write out an exercise that you can practice when facing the situation.

A. Activating event: write what happened.

B. Belief about the event: describe your belief about what happened.

C. Change the way I see it: Can you change your belief about what happened? Describe an example of this event and how you can use RET to resolve your stress about it.

For example: consider fear over political unrest in the country you're serving.

A. Activating event: You're faced with political unrest.

B. Belief about the event: "We will never get out of the country. We could die or be taken prisoner."

C. How can I change my belief and calm my anxiety? As a Christian, I can say that I believe that I have an appointed time to die, which is not today.

> **Use the lines below to write out several anxieties/fears and describe how you would use RET to resolve them.**

____

____

____

____

____

____

____

____

____

____

Remember, knowledge is power. The more you ask the Holy Spirit to point out the stressors and allow His strength and grace to lift your depression, trauma, anxiety, and stress, the more it will help. Also, the Lord will help you connect the dots when your anxiety or depression may be connected to some trauma. So, take the knowledge you've learned about yourself when working with Rational Emotive Therapy.

Once again, Ellis's Emotive Therapy consists of three steps: an *activating event* (what happened), *your belief about the event* (your belief about what happened), and your work to *change the way you see the event to resolve your stress about it.* As a second exercise, consider a situation where you must leave a secure, safe homeland to serve in a different country with an unfamiliar culture.

A. Activating event: you're leaving a secure home and going to an unfamiliar place.

B. Belief about the event: I may never adjust or something awful might happen to me or my family.

C. How can I change my belief and calm my anxiety? As a Christian I can say that I believe God has called me and will give me the requisite equipment and protection to do His work.

Use the lines on the next page to write out several anxieties/fears, and describe how you would use RET to resolve them.

Write several situations where you can use RET.

Remember how Brad's sense of smell triggered a severe panic attack due to smelling urine and feces in the ballpark bathroom. Now see if you can recall a scent or something you heard or saw that could have elicited a sense of anxiety in you that you can relate to a trauma you have experienced on or off the mission field. Then, please write your experience below.

Having the ability to identify an acute sensory experience—whether of smell, hearing, seeing, or some other sense—you will be able to connect it with an incident of buried trauma and thereby control your reaction.

List the things that have created anxiety for you on the mission field.

What revelations have you discovered about yourself, given what you've read up to now, and your answers to the above questions?

What do you feel you can change going forward that will not interfere with your ability to live a life that is freer of depression, stress, and trauma upon staying in your homeland?

As a result of working on the training sessions and workbook, what has better prepared you to return to the mission field?

CHAPTER EIGHT:
Trauma Recovery Using Dialectical Behavioral Therapy (DBT)

Trauma has a way of visiting us daily unless we can develop tools to help us maintain our distance from it. The practice of DBT will enable the victim to practice DBT until it becomes a conditioned response to the visuals of trauma that often plague the mind. The exercises below practiced on a daily basis will become an automatic response to the trauma images that are imprinted on the brain. The missionary will also be able to use these practices on the population they serve, especially for those that have experienced trauma, depression, and anxiety from having to escape political unrest in their country.

Four modules:

- Core mindfulness: Being aware of what is happening in the present.

- Distress tolerance: Lowering the stress or feeling of panic.

- Emotion regulation: Being conscious of how you're feeling i.e. angry, overly stressed, or sad.

- Interpersonal effectiveness: How we can project a different outcome when dealing with ourselves and others.

These are designed to assist individuals in better managing behaviors, emotions, and thoughts.

Erica Laub has explained that DBT consists of eight different steps.

- Mindfulness: Being aware of cues, triggers, and feelings without judging yourself.

- Distress tolerance: Learning to tolerate stress so we don't make a stressful situation worse.

- Emotional regulation: Effectively managing emotions. See also 2 Timothy 1:7: "For God has not given us a spirit of timidity, but a spirit of power, of love, and of self-discipline."

- Interpersonal effectiveness: Teaching people to cope with conflict and build healthy relationships. See also James 1 19:20: "My dear brothers, take note of this: be quick to listen, slow to speak, and slow to become angry, for a man's anger does not bring about the righteous life God desires."

- Exposure and response prevention: Using light exposure to eliminate unhealthy response or unwanted behaviors, such as avoidance.

- Opposite action: Recognizing your personal "action urge" associated with experience. For example, unpleasant experiences give you the need to run.

- Validation: Knowing that your life experiences are your truth. People with PTSD may question their own reality and what happened to them because the stress and pain can feel hard to tolerate.

- Self-acceptance: Accepting that pain does not always have to mean suffering; refusing to be okay with being hurt, abused, or traumatized. You can overcome what happened to you by taking back control, managing the emotions as they come, and allowing yourself to feel and heal. The trauma is not going away but you can learn to live with it, and not have it sabotage the good experiences in life. Philippians 4 11:14: "I am not saying this because I am in need, for I have learned to be content whatever the circumstances. I know what it is to be in need, and I know what it is to have plenty. I have learned the secret of being content in any and every situation, whether living in plenty or in want. I can do everything through him who gives me strength."

What are some examples of emotions that you feel need regulation?

____

____

____

____

____

Give some examples of ways you can use DBT to help regulate your emotions listed on the above lines.

____

____

____

____

____

____

____

____

____

____

____

____

____

Can you identify certain triggers that may cause unease in your life? For example, Michael could identify the burning body smell or similar smells that caused him anxiety. Use the workbook lines below to identify them.

____

____

____

____

____

____

____

____

____

____

____

____

____

Can you identify those triggers, cues, or feelings that have the fight or flight response?

Once you have identified the things that cause you to feel a fight or flight response, come up with a plan for staying in the feelings and not running from the mission field. You can use any of the therapies or any of the imaginary techniques to implement.

Again, a look at Rational Emotive Therapy to practice protocol for dealing with others who are experiencing trauma.

Ross and Brenda Robinson are a missionary couple who have been involved in Moldova, where many Ukrainian immigrants have traveled to escape their war-torn country. The Robinsons have recognized the need for trauma counseling. They understand that any of the therapies can be used to help alleviate the anxiety and fear of being traumatized. CBT, DBT, and RET are suggested when dealing with a population that has had terrible trauma due to the ravages of war. The trauma leaves an indelible imprint on the brain, and those images cause anxiety, depression, and a trauma response, such as panic attacks. Refugees of war don't typically know how to deal with their own trauma. But missionaries not only equip themselves but teach populations that have been displaced by war.

You can ask the group you're serving to take each incident and describe how they could deal with the flashbacks and the triggers for their post-traumatic stress. You can help them by using CBT and/or DBT.

When talking with missionary couples who have been involved in Moldova where a number of Ukraine immigrants have left their war-torn country to enter into Moldova, they have recognized the need for trauma counseling. Then any of the therapies can be used to help alleviate the anxiety and fear of being traumatized.

Write below examples of situations in your country of service how you feel the people you serve can benefit from the therapies of CBT, DBT, and RET.

CHAPTER NINE:
Loneliness

Lastly, the feeling of loneliness that is never really addressed. Loneliness may be glossed over but with little or no protocol for wellness.

How do we combat loneliness on the mission field? One of my favorite missionary biographies is about a missionary named John Paton. John Paton was a missionary to the New Hebrides Islands of the South Pacific. When John Paton was burdened to go and take the gospel to the unreached people in the South Seas, he received great resistance from many in his church. One elder told him, "You will be eaten by cannibals." Paton responded, "Mr. Dickson, you are advanced in years now, and your own prospect is soon to be laid in the grave, there to be eaten by worms; I confess to you, that if I can but live and die serving and honoring the Lord Jesus, it will make no difference to me whether I am eaten by cannibals or by worms."

When Paton landed on the mission field, he experienced a time of loneliness. How did he deal with his loneliness? He reveals this to us in his autobiography. One night he was being chased by natives, who were trying to kill him. To avoid them, he climbed into a tree, where he would spend many hours alone. "I climbed into the tree," he noted, "and was there left alone in the bush. The hours I spent there live all before me as if it were yesterday. I heard the frequent discharge of muskets, and the yells of the savages. Yet I sat there among the branches, as safe in the arms of Jesus! Never, in all my sorrows did my Lord draw nearer to me, and speak more soothingly to my soul, than when the moonlight flickered among these chestnut leaves, and the night air played on my throbbing brow, as I told all my heart to Jesus. Alone, yet not alone! If it be to glorify my God, I will not grudge to spend many nights alone in such a tree, to feel again my Savior's spiritual presence, to enjoy His consoling fellowship."

Paton used imagery to get him through a time of trauma and loneliness. We can hide in our hearts and minds many scriptures to get us through lonely times. One can only imagine how lonely unbelievers must feel in times of trouble, but believers like John Paton felt total comfort in the arms of Jesus. A scripture to hide in your heart when you feel alone would be: Psalm 63 vs. 7 "Because you are my help, my soul clings to you; Your right hand upholds me. Imagine clinging to our Lord, who never leaves us and imagining Him holding on to us in the palm of His hand."

Paton battled his loneliness and suffering by spending time with God and drawing closer to Him. Paul was frequented with loneliness: Paul writes to Timothy. "Do your best to come to me soon. For Demas, in love with the present world, has deserted me and gone to Thessalonica. Crescens had gone to Galatia, Titus to Dalmatia. Luke alone is with me. Get Mark and bring him with you, for he is very useful to me for ministry. Tychicus I have sent to Ephesus. When you come, bring the cloak that I left with Carpus at Troas, also the books, and above all the parchments" (2 Timothy 4:9-13). At the time of writing these lines, Paul was under Roman arrest and sentenced to die (2 Timothy 4:6). He was practically alone, having only Luke with him. He wrote to Timothy, his spiritual son, to come and see him. Paul seemed to be experiencing sadness and loneliness and he desperately needed to see Timothy and spend time with him. One of his fellow laborers in the ministry, Demas, had fallen in love with the world and deserted Paul.

How do we combat loneliness on and off the mission field?

- Use Paton's example of asking the Lord to comfort you on all sides. Consider the verse John 14:14: "You may ask for anything in my name and I will do it." Jesus doesn't say He *may* do it, but that He *will*. When you are lonely, ask the Lord to comfort you, and try to feel His presence.

- Always have a prayer partner with you on the mission field like the Apostle Paul who realized a Christian partner helped with loneliness.

- Use mindfulness to redirect any feelings of emptiness. Direct your thoughts to a beautiful site in nature.

- Use a repeated mantra. For example, thank the Lord for all your blessings by naming them one by one.

- Recite a favorite verse.

- Try to distinguish between depression and loneliness. Depression is loss of joy in everything, so when we suggest more socialization, the depressed person wants to isolate. Loneliness can be 1) *emotional* loneliness, which is the absence of meaningful relationships; 2) *social* loneliness, which is a perceived deficit in the quality of social connections; 3) *existential* loneliness, which is a feeling of fundamental separateness from others in the wider world. All three can be experienced when missionaries enter into a different culture and language.

- Sometimes depression and loneliness can overlap. Depression will be dealt with differently than loneliness. Michael and Samantha talked about leaving behind Christian friends in Nepal, where they had experienced a warm fellowship. They experienced a deep sense of loss, which is loneliness.

- Try to develop human contact with someone other than your spouse on a regular basis, no matter if you are in or out of the field. Pray that the Lord will help you connect with someone who is like-minded.

- Use the space below to write a detailed plan describing how you are going to alleviate feelings of loneliness, both abroad and at home in the United States.

In conclusion, we have developed a protocol for mental health wellness for the missionary, but also for the population they are working with in any region—especially a displaced people from a war-torn country. This protocol for healing is a way for the missionary to not only use these therapies for their own wellness but for the wellness of those they serve.

As a result of working on the training session of *Mental Health Care for Global Missionaries*, do you feel you're better prepared to return to the mission field? Describe your changing feelings and mindset in the journal lines below, by looking at and working through the depression, anxiety, loneliness, and trauma you have experienced on and off the mission field.

Godspeed in the days ahead.